GRIEVING THROUGH GRACE

A guide to the grief journey after the loss of a child or loved one!

by Jamie Dickerson

The contents of this work, including, but not limited to, the accuracy of events, people, and places depicted; opinions expressed; permission to use previously published materials included; and any advice given or actions advocated are solely the responsibility of the author, who assumes all liability for said work and indemnifies the publisher against any claims stemming from publication of the work.

All Rights Reserved
Copyright © 2024 by Jamie Dickerson

No part of this book may be reproduced or transmitted, downloaded, distributed, reverse engineered, or stored in or introduced into any information storage and retrieval system, in any form or by any means, including photocopying and recording, whether electronic or mechanical, now known or hereinafter invented without permission in writing from the publisher.

Dorrance Publishing Co
585 Alpha Drive
Pittsburgh, PA 15238
Visit our website at *www.dorrancebookstore.com*

ISBN: 979-8-89211-172-0
eISBN: 979-8-89211-670-1

As everyone else's lives go on as normal, mine seems to stand still. Every minute of every day searching for answers as to why and how to keep my child's memory alive. I look around and pictures are everywhere of her face. I look outside and see peace but feel so broken. The pain is unexplainable, and unless people have experienced the loss of a child, there is no way to relate. I think to myself, God had to watch Jesus die, suffering and yelling out, "Why have you forsaken me?" As I sat there at my daughter's hospital bed, I felt that same way. I felt forsaken and forgotten. I was quickly reminded by the scripture I have stored up in my heart that it is not my timing but God's. 2 Peter 3:8 says, "But do not forget this one thing, dear friends: With the Lord a day is like a thousand years, and a thousand years are like a day." Again in Ecclesiastes 3:1-8 we are reminded,

"There is a time for everything, and a season for every activity under the heavens: A time to be born and a time to die, a time to plant and a time to uproot, a time to kill and a time to heal, a time to tear down and a time to build, a time to weep and a time to laugh, a time to mourn and a time to dance, a time to scatter stones and a time to gather them, a time to embrace and a time to refrain from embracing, a time to search and a time to give up, a time to keep and a time to throw away, a time to tear and a time to mend, a time to be silent and a time to speak, a time to love and a time to hate, a time for war and a time for peace."

God prepared me for this moment by giving the Holy Spirit to tap into and rely on. For days I have walked around numb, feelings of high emotions and low emotions. Feelings of anger and hurt. People often mention my strength through these times and my only answer is that I am not walking in flesh but in spirit. My flesh is not strong enough for such a time as this!

My twenty-nine-year-old daughter April Lynn Holt passed away just eight days ago on July 31, 2023.

At 4:13 p.m. on July 19, 2023, I received the call that would change my life forever. As I answered the phone, all I heard was my son-in-law on the other end of the phone hysterical telling me that he had found my daughter April in the shower; she was not breathing, and is being taken to the nearest hospital by ambulance. I jumped in my car without a moment's thought. I even left my husband and granddaughter at home while in such a rush to get to the hospital which was over an hour away from my house.

When I arrived at the hospital, I felt in my gut something was wrong, seriously wrong. I felt a piece of me had gone somewhere but I was not sure where or what had left my body. A feeling I have never experienced before. I didn't even hastily walk into the hospital but rather walked slowly dreading every step I took, and as I got closer to the door that feeling got even stronger. They were not allowing anyone back to see her and again I knew something was not right; something was very wrong. When they called us back to a room labeled C5, again I knew something was not right; something was very wrong. It felt like eternity for the doctor to come in that room. I was curled into a ball on a bench feeling as though I was going to vomit. My cries were loud enough to be heard in the rooms adjacent. As a mother I had the worst feeling that I would walk out of that room with a piece of my heart gone forever. The doctor came in the room, squatted down, spoke directly and with little compassion, and told me my daughter went without oxygen and blood flow for at least 15 minutes and most likely longer. If she was to wake up, she would have severe brain damage. He told me she wasn't showing any brain activity or blood flow to her brain. They would give her a fighting chance though and they put her on life support. So, for the next three days I sat by her side in the CCU. I held her hand, I shouted out to her, I played music for her, I prayed fervently over her body, I rubbed her forehead, and kissed her. With each touch and each kiss, I knew in my heart her soul was no longer in there. The body lying there was the flesh of my baby girl. The flesh that I held, I rocked, I raised, and that God allowed me to be the mother of.

With each test the doctor took, nothing was good news other than her organs staying alive. I would grab her hand and her body was cold as ice. They would then pack her body with more ice on her inner thighs and under her arms due to her internal temperature being high. I thought to myself of all those years I would take her to the grocery store as a little girl and she would freeze. She would always tell me, "Mommy, I'm so cold." Even as an adult when she would come over to visit, she would wear one of my sweaters or use a blanket because she was always cold. I wanted so badly to wrap her body in a blanket and warm her up. I remember vividly how I would peel back her eyelids and look into my baby's beautiful brown eyes and knew her soul was not there. There was nobody looking back at me. I have never experienced such a thing in my life. I have never looked into the eyes of someone that I love so much and them not being in their fleshly body. Her dad would sit by her side and wipe the drainage coming from her tubes down her neck. I remember him placing a towel under her cheek and standing over her talking to her with all the love in the world for his baby girl. We prayed over her, we called out to her, we wept over her body. As his little girl laid there, he had so much hope in his heart, he had a hope that I did not feel.

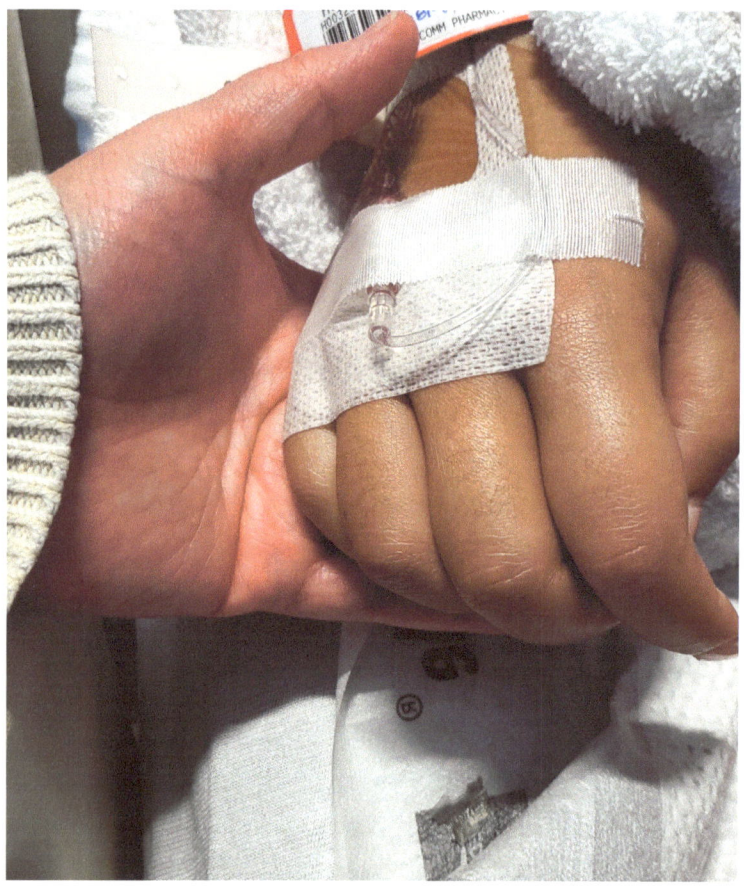

Nonetheless, we sat there with faith that God could save her if it was His will to do so, but my mamma gut was continually reminded that I was just sitting with her fleshly body and not her soul. The child I hugged, raised, loved, would do anything for was no longer there and I didn't know how I would go on without her. I was breathless. My legs couldn't stand. My heart literally hurt with chest pains, and I wailed, and I wailed while laying on her body. I laid there rubbing her face and listening to her heartbeat. That moment was the most insufficient and helpless moment that I have ever felt in my entire life. I couldn't make my baby better. Everything was out of my hands. I remember leaving that room and looking back one last time and thinking that is the last moment I will ever see her physical form again. Her head lying to the side, her body was completely limp, but she was still as beautiful as ever. I went to the hallway and leaned on the wall while my legs wanted to give out from under me. I couldn't walk,

I needed to be held up. I felt like my life was being taken from me. I had to tell myself to breathe in and breathe out. I did all of this without my husband because he had just left the hospital one hour prior to go home and care for the dogs. I called him begging him to come back but at the same time barely able to speak. He turned around immediately and came back to the hospital. He was broken, he was suffering too right along with me. We leaned into each other in disbelief that we were going through a moment such as this. I was begging for an empty room to grieve in and sign the forms needed to leave because I could not re-enter the room with my daughter in it. The hospital kindly sent me to the fifth floor, into a room in the corner where I crawled up into the hospital bed in the fetal position and just wanted to stop breathing. The whole world seemed to have paused for a moment. I always wondered how people handle the news that their child passed away. I stared at the walls in a daze. I almost felt nothing, nothing at all. I couldn't feel anything other than my heart beating out of my chest. After the papers were signed, I knew leaving the hospital would be the last time I saw my daughter. As we slowly walked to the car, I slumped into the passenger seat. All I could do is cry out, "Why, Lord, why my baby?" I will never understand until I stand before God one day myself. I have no choice to accept God calling her home.

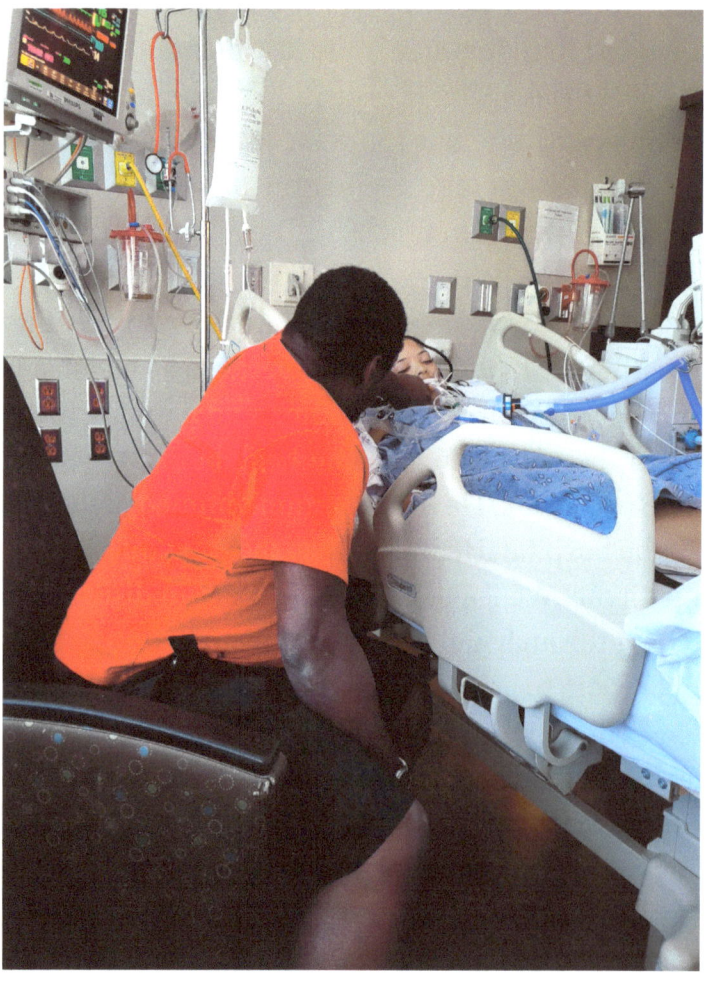

Several days have passed and I am now ready to share with the world how this grieving through grace process is the only way to make it through such tragedy and loss.

It is now day nine, and the grieving process is something I haven't experienced before. I feel so many emotions in one day. My tone in my voice is even different. If I could describe the feeling it would be if your electricity went out and you were then running on a generator. God is my generator and recharging me continuously to keep me running. Without Him the electricity would be off right now. Jesus Christ paid this light bill a long time ago by the giving of His life for us to have eternal life. My lights aren't off because the bill wasn't paid. The lights are off because of a storm and in time that energy will turn back on, but until then the generator will keep it going. This is not just any storm but a cyclone. One that comes to kill and take any and everything out in its path. The Bible tells us in John 10:10, "The thief comes only to steal and kill and destroy." I must remind myself this pain is not from God but from the enemy. I sit here with my seven-year-old grandson with his head in his lap crying for his mom. He doesn't understand why his mom is gone and is crying out for her. He wails that all that is left is her spirit and I sit here not knowing what to say. I prayed over him and am begging God to send us peace. I pray that in the morning we find peace in unexpected places and that his heart be happy. Until tomorrow I will fill myself with scripture to make it through another day. My day nine advice: It is okay to NOT be okay!

Day ten is here. One more day without my baby girl. Today I tried to focus on what plans I had with my daughter. A few months ago, we sat together, and we planned to create an umbrella company named "He Reigns". The meaning behind the name is that just like an umbrella protecting us from a storm, Christ protects us through all of life's storms. I never in a million years would have imagined that the storm I would be going through would be this very one and that she wouldn't be here by my side. We never got to see those plans through so today I picked myself up and I went to a local store that rents out retail spaces and I signed up for a space. I am very excited to see one of our plans come to life in her honor. Ultimately "He Reigns" and His will is what I seek each day. Grieving through grace is pushing past the devil's intentions of pulling me down to the pits of hell. Grieving through grace means I will see God's grace even through the rain clouds. I know that the storm I am in will turn into a beautiful rainbow. This pain must turn to reflection of all the good times. The Lord showed me grace by letting me be April's mom. I had 29 years with her. Although 29 years is not near enough, I am so grateful for each moment I had with her. Last year April decided to go on two trips with us as a family which she hasn't done in years. We all often focus on the material aspects of life and what we want more of, and yet the person taking their last breath only wants more time. How we spend our time and who we spend our time with is really all that matters. Today I listened to a sermon on Job and reminded myself that God is not the one causing such heartache. I need to turn to God for my strength and thank Him for the 29 years that I had to experience life with April. My day ten advice: Think back to one thing you wished you would have done together or planned to do together and plan to live it out. Your loved one's spirit will be right there with you, and this will fill you with joy. In addition, read through the book of Job and stand firm in your faith.

    We have made it to day eleven and this has been a day accepting what I cannot change. We had family members clean out our daughter's apartment, bring her things to our home, and put them in our garage. I could not get myself to be there to go through her things or see where she was found. To be honest I don't even want to drive the direction of her home. However, the thought that she would need clothes to be buried in never crossed my mind and so when they called to have us bring clothes to the funeral home, I couldn't even go in my garage to find clothes. Her dad did it for me, praise God. He chose her a comfortable outfit that she wore often; he even got her underwear and a bra. You never know when a breakdown moment will appear, and so when we drove the clothes up to funeral home, we noticed we forgot socks. There it was another breakdown moment for me. I hysterically cried and took off my socks, and unbeknownst to me, I had mismatched socks on that day which made me cry even more. My husband offered to drive me up to the store to buy new socks, but I wailed, "No, I want her to wear my mismatched socks, the ones that were on her mom's feet." So, my husband brought them inside and yes, my baby was buried in her mommy's mismatched socks.

Back to accepting the things I cannot change, today I had to face the items in my garage. It was not my choice to go through her things so soon. However, her eleven-year-old daughter wanted to have her purses, which then turned into her shoes, and then into her clothes. As the bags of items were brought in, I put on a brave face knowing that this may be her daughter's way of grieving. She hasn't shown much emotion to this point and so when she asks to do anything regarding her mom, I pull up my big girl pants and do it. As she poured the clothes on the floor, I picked up a shirt and held it so close to my face, clenching onto it I just started crying as I could smell my daughter. I hugged the shirt not wanting to let it go. I was not prepared for this moment. I was not prepared for her scent. I was not prepared to see her worn shoes and know she had walked through life in them. Nonetheless, I had to face what was before me. As the day wore on, I watched my granddaughter smile and try on her mom's clothes and shoes. Her smile made my heart happy. I could see my daughter in my granddaughter, and it reminded me that her legacy will live on through her children. My day eleven advice: take time to grieve but don't hold yourself back from the fear of having to face uncomfortable moments. Those moments will be hard, very hard; however, those moments will help in the healing process and can bring peace and show us ways to reflect and keep their memory alive. I plan to take some of my daughter's clothes and make myself and her two children quilts so that when they are wrapped up in them, they will feel her hugs. In addition, I will be using some of her shirts to make Christmas ornaments for the people who were close to her to give away during the holidays. Lastly, since she journaled daily, her thoughts and words are on paper, so I plan to frame a few of her entries. I will cherish these journals always.

    Day twelve feels like day 150. Today I focused on moving past the urge to withdraw from others! My mind is exhausted with thoughts that I can't turn off and I am finding them consuming me. If my thoughts were a plant, they would be a kudzu lianas vine. A kudzu liana will triumph in a forest and steal the water and nutrients from surrounding trees and plants eventually killing them. My thoughts are attempting to steal my joy and trying to attack my faith by intertwining my knowledge with my doubt. I know God will give me strength daily, but doubt makes me second guess I have that strength I need to function daily. As I lay in bed thinking to myself that I don't want to get up, I fight the urge to cover my head with blankets and lay in the dark. I made myself get up. I then convinced myself to get some cleaning done, which after a week and a half was very needed. I planned on staying in the house today, but after cleaning my husband insisted that we get some fresh air and go for a drive. As resistant as I was, I can say the drive was good for me. Different scenery than staring at my walls was a nice change. By allowing him to see a need that I didn't know I needed at the time I was able to get some well needed sunshine and a reset of my mindset. My day twelve advice is to allow others to see a need and fill it for you without your resistance. Go outside and allow the sun to penetrate you with the vitamins you need and take some deep breaths of fresh air. As those vines try to take over your mindset, continue to cut them back by reading scripture, reversing your thoughts to positive memories, and seeking out other areas of your life that you see blessings. Bad thoughts turn into bad attitudes and bad attitudes turn into resentment and anger which is exactly what the devil wants. We can fight that warfare with a much mightier force and that is God. Allow Him to fight this battle, hand Him the weapons that you have stored up in your soul and He will not forsake you. We are only ready to stand and take on the battle after we have knelt down and been given the strength and armor needed for the fight ahead of us.

Thirteen days have come and gone since the passing of my daughter. No day has seemed normal yet and I can still say I am not okay. I have accepted that this feeling of a hole within my heart is now a piece of me. No doctor, surgeon, or human can repair the hole.

God will keep it bandaged so I can keep moving forward.

Every Sunday for years now I have had family dinner at our house and all the kids and grandkids are invited. Some weeks it will be all of them, and others depending on their schedules it might only be a few of them. Regardless I still had dinner and love this time set aside for my family. Having grown children who work and have families of their own means squeezing in time with them can be difficult, so knowing once per week I get time spent just enjoying one another means so much to me. Today was the first Sunday dinner I had without being able to invite my daughter. It was very hard for me to do, but I know I can't stop spending time and creating memories with my other children and grandchildren. I placed her picture in the center of the kitchen island and throughout the day reminded myself she is still with us all in our hearts. My two-year-old granddaughter did a fashion show with all my daughter's purses. She would prance through the living room and show them to us with a huge smile on her face. I pray April was looking down and enjoying the show with a smile on her face as well.

My day thirteen advice would be surround yourself with the people you love and don't be offended if they are not grieving the same as you. As I watch my grown sons continue with life, I feel a bit hurt that they don't grieve the same as me. Every thought I have is about my daughter and I still sit numb for a lot of my day. I watch the two of them laughing and loving life and I know it is not because they don't miss their sister. I am aware each person grieves differently, and I wouldn't want them to sit and feel the pain I am feeling. I am accepting that some people avoid the topic because it is too uncomfortable, or they just don't know what to say. Others say things and don't realize some of the words are trigger words for my emotions. For example, my mom called an invited "my whole" family over for dinner next weekend. The word whole is like a two-edged sword cutting right through me seeing as I will never have my whole family together again. My mom wouldn't have even thought that a word could be a trigger for me and yet it brings me to tears to think my daughter won't be there. How I perceive something is not the intentions of the deliverer. Who would even think a word could bring me to tears. During this fragile time of healing, allowing myself to recognize that we all grieve differently is essential to showing grace to everyone where they are, as well as giving myself space for grace to shine through.

Two weeks have come and gone. I have survived two weeks without one of my children. I feel like time is standing still and that my feet are frozen. My son said something to me, and it stuck; he said, "You can take as much time as you need as long as you keep moving forward." In my mind I don't feel like I am moving forward; nonetheless, with every second that passes, I am breathing in and out and I am getting up and taking part in my day, and therefore I am moving forward one second at a time. Giving ourselves grace during this time allows us to slow the pace of life down to a comfortable speed. Moving too fast will only cause a cover-up of emotions that will compile into many problems down the road. Moving too slowly will allow depression to set in and steal our blessings by pulling us back from everything we love. The balance of healing at a safe pace is essential to the mental health of a grieving person. I gauge daily what my mental health is looking like. I ask myself on a scale of one too ten with ten being the happiest what am I feeling. Today, day fourteen, I would say I am at a four. This is an activity I do with my loved ones as well on a regular basis. It's okay to have bad days especially during a tragedy such as losing a child or any loved one. However, if weeks go by as that number goes lower or even stays the same, I will know that medical attention is needed to help me/my loved one get through that season in life. Therefore, my day fourteen advice is to evaluate your mental health daily. Keep a journal or jot down on your calendar what your number is each day to keep track. Keep your daily vitamins balanced and focus on a personal hour for just you. This time can be spent working out, sitting on your porch swing, reading scripture, taking a hot bath, doing yoga, meditating on God's word, going on a walk, or any means of uninterrupted relaxing for you.

Fifteen days in, I made it past the two-week mark. Looking for a purpose to continue is a way to press through the excruciating pain daily. I have my daughter's two children ages seven and eleven with me. I homeschool them; therefore, daily we have a schedule and a routine that helps us all distract our minds from the events encircling us. We took two weeks off, and although I could probably take a year off, I needed to get back to a daily routine.

Do you ever think about what legacy you will leave behind? I do. I wonder what impact I have made on other people. Anyone that knew my daughter would say she had the kindest heart and most gentle spirit. I remind her children each day how their mom will live through them. We don't reflect on the bad traits, what someone owned, how much money was in their bank account, what their sins were, or what they didn't accomplish when someone we love passes away. We focus on where their heart was, how was their walk with the Lord, and how we can keep their legacy alive. We cherish our time with them and look back at moments when life had slowed down, and we created those moments to "just be" together. If I could get anything back with my daughter, it would be more time. I would have asked her to have lunch/coffee more. I would have planned that mommy daughter trip that we had talked about for years. I would have told her how proud I was of her more often. I would never have left a visit without a hug. Time would be what I would want back. One more look into her beautiful brown eyes and one more time to see her amazing smile. Her seven-year-old son loves to get his back scratched and that is one thing his mom would do every day for him. So, as I am typing with one hand, I am scratching his back with my other. I won't pass up these moments. My advice for day fifteen would be to look around you, evaluate who those people in your life are that make an impact on you and then focus your attention on spending intentional time with them because once they are gone, so is that opportunity.

Sixteen days into grieving, today I took my grandson to visit his mom's grave. As we put two solar sunflower lights out there and prayed over her, I just started crying, okay bawling. The thought that the body that I hugged for 29 years was under the ground is surreal. My grandson crouched down next to his mom's grave saying, "I just wish my mom was still alive." We walked around the graveyard reading the headstones of many people. We would talk about the ages of other people that have passed; surprisingly many of them were younger in years. The graveyard we chose to bury our daughter in is very peaceful. Approximately one month ago my mom had called me and asked me if I wanted to meet her at a graveyard right down the road from our church to choose a gravesite for my grandma. My grandma has had dementia for quite a while now and is in hospice in a nearby nursing home. We want to be prepared for her passing, seeing as that seems to be soon. I met my mom and dad at the graveyard, we pulled in, and a very kind gentleman met us there who helps in finding a place of rest for your loved one. He knew stories about so many of the people that were buried there, including his dad. He gave us peace in choosing a beautiful site. At that moment my mom asked me what I thought about just buying two sites since our family is so large and I said, "Sure, that would be a good idea." The sites were purchased, and we didn't think anything more about the timing of the Lord at that moment. When my daughter passed, and all the final arrangements had to be made, we knew that God had us choose those two sites for this very reason. In all the chaos and heartache, I had peace about where to bury my child. I knew where she would be. The day of the funeral I still felt that overwhelming peace at that cemetery and today when we went to visit, I reflected on how God aligned everything. As we sat at April's grave, a blue dragonfly approached us. This beautiful creature was flying back and forth within inches of landing on us. It hovered around as if it were looking right in our eyes.

It would land on the grave right next to us as if it was having a visit. When we left so did the dragonfly. Later when I returned home, I looked up the meaning of a blue dragonfly that visits a grave. It was interesting that many believe that the blue dragonfly signifies a connection with the spirit world. This could very well be a myth; however, that beautiful dragonfly brought peace to my heart. We so often don't think about the moments we are living in, and that God already knows the plans for us. Don't pass up your opportunities that God is aligning you with to give you strength for another moment in life. Storing up scripture, walking with God daily, and cherishing the minutes of each day is what will get you through during the toughest times in life. Tragedy is not something we are ever ready for! Our flesh will react out of emotion unless we are grounded in God's word! My advice for day sixteen is to reflect on how God prepared you for this moment. Take time to pray for continued guidance and grace.

    Day seventeen's lesson is don't forget your morning coffee time! This might sound quite funny to most people. In saying don't miss the morning coffee, what I am getting at is a morning routine of showing yourself some self-love and self-compassion each day is essential. I haven't been able to wake up yet in a happy, excited mood like I used to. I probably won't be able to for quite some time. When your heart is broken, it takes time to heal. My mom had open heart surgery and needed a quadruple bypass suddenly with no prior signs at the age of 59. When she woke up from surgery, she needed a lot of assistance; she needed to slowly get back to her daily activities and that took months, not days. To this day she will say that she is not 100% back to who she was before the heart surgery. The scar she has running down her chest is a symbol of what she has been through. I believe losing a child is much like that healing process. My heart is broken into a million pieces and feels like it was ripped out of my chest at times. I give myself grace knowing it has only been seventeen days since her passing. However, I am very aware that this will take a lifetime of healing and I will never be the same. I will still live my life as God intended me to do so and will seek His purpose continuously in my life. However, the pain I am experiencing will be bandaged with the Holy Spirit but if you peak under that bandage, you will always see the scar. The advice I would give for day seventeen is to show yourself the grace and compassion needed to heal. Take time each day to allow yourself to sip some coffee and reflect on those memories that were given to you no matter how many of them you have tucked away in your heart. Showing compassion to ourselves is just as important as showing compassion to others.

Day eighteen would be the day of, be prepared for anything! Today I woke up and started my day out by having to go choose a headstone for my daughter. When I entered the funeral home, a lady approached me, and I awkwardly leaned in for a hug when she clearly was not. So, we ended up doing some weird side hug that was just not even supposed to happen. I guess my mind assumed everyone wanted to hug me since I am grieving, forgetting that not everyone even knows what I am going through. I then proceeded to write a check for a ridiculous amount because I wanted something beautiful for my beautiful daughter on her gravesite. While writing the check, I just started telling this lady all about what had happened. She stood there and listened to me go on and on for quite a while. Suddenly I realized she was just waiting for the check so she could make a copy. I left there thinking to myself not everyone I encounter is going to be grieving with me and 99% of society won't even understand what it feels like to bury a child. I must prepare myself for this, so I don't become offended. There are people very close to me that don't seem to let their days even be disrupted by my tragedy. I am living this nightmare every second of my day and people around me, even my loved ones, are just going about life. I almost get mad at people having a good time, laughing, or if they even mention my daughter's name in any way other than putting her on a pedestal. Coming to grips with the fact that she was my daughter, she came from my womb, my body was attached to hers like nobody else could ever be is something that separates me from the rest of the grieving.

Being prepared for moments of sudden sadness is normal too. Today we went to a friend's house for dinner. As I was driving home, the expressway ramp happened to be shut down, so it forced me to go another route. I didn't think much of it and as I am driving, I realize I am headed straight towards the cemetery that my daughter is buried in. It is pitch black outside, and two days ago I went and put solar light sunflowers on her grave. As I approach the cemetery on my left-hand side, I just start bawling my eyes out. I felt like my daughter, the child I had held as a baby, the body I have loved on for 29 years was laying lonely in a dark cemetery. She was all by herself, and I couldn't go be with her. I couldn't stop her from being alone in the dark. I couldn't say goodnight even one more time. I wasn't prepared for that moment like I was a few days prior when I went there to visit. There will be times when circumstances arise that will strike an emotion that will cause a breakdown. This can happen anywhere and at any time. Let those emotions flow, let yourself not be okay for a moment.

As I said, day eighteen has been a day of not being prepared for random emotions.

After I went to the funeral home, I went by the craft store. As I walked into the store, they called for another cashier to come to the front to assist customers and the name they called over the intercom just happened to be my daughter's name, April. I took a deep breath and kept walking. I went down the candle aisle and I saw a candle named Sugar Rose. I knew my daughter's favorite smell was rose. I picked up the candle and stood there just smelling it and crying. Everything around me reminds me of her: smells, tv shows, songs, pictures, places, etc. As life continues to go on day by day, minute by minute, and second by second just be prepared for the unexpected moments that will creep up on you. My day eighteen advice is to allow yourself those moments and allow yourself to remember your loved one through every opportunity you get. One day those tears will turn to smiles of remembering all the good memories you have. I can't wait for that day to come!

Day nineteen, and if I had to describe my emotions on a scale of one to ten with ten being feeling great, I would give myself a four today. Just kind of woke up feeling down. I don't feel depressed, I just feel sad. When I go to bed at night, my hopes are to wake up and feel energized and I haven't experienced that morning yet. The day was just getting started and I already knew what was ahead of me. Today was our first family event since April passed that she was not going to be at. I dreaded having to face that. I dreaded having her children attend a family event and not having parents there to run to like all of the other kids in the family. I didn't want them to feel displaced or for people to look at me with pity. I also am not that social these days. I like solitary moments, and during long conversations I tend to zone out. Coming off rude is the last thing I want to do; therefore, I try hard to put a smile on my face, put my thoughts on a back burner, and let the moment go on with me being as present as I can. It is August and knowing the holidays are right around the corner and April won't be there for the first time in 29 years is something right now I can't wrap my head around. I will have to approach each holiday just like I did today. When we arrived at the event, I could see my grandson did not know who to turn to in order to ask for help. Immediately I called him over to me and told him me and his poppy are right there and anything he needs he just needs to come to us. I also reminded him that the gift I had brought had his name and his sister's name on the card. He ran off and played and would come back from time to time to sit near me. My granddaughter, well she is eleven, she just wanted to play and have fun. My grandson's birthday is in October and my daughter has always made him feel so special. I am already trying to think of ways to make sure he feels that way this year too. Today I had to face an obstacle of the lack of presence of my daughter for the first time. As much as it tempted me to stay home, I am very glad that I went and faced the situation at hand. Now the first time is over. The second time won't be as hard and so forth and so forth. There are people still celebrating. Life continues to move forward even when my world stands still, and if I allow my mind to stay standing still, I won't be in the headspace to take on God's purpose. My day nineteen advice would be to face those giants head on one by one. Bring your weapon of the strength of the Holy Spirit to carry you through each of them. It won't be easy. It will never be the same; nonetheless, through the different and awkward moments we must seek God's grace and peace for our lives and the others around us that need us.

Sunday is here; twenty days have come and gone.

Twenty sunrises and sunsets have come and gone. 28,800 minutes have come and gone without my child. Our church family has been amazing throughout this time. A little bit about myself is that I am a youth director for our church. My daughter that passed away taught with me in my classrooms and the kids loved her. Everyone always asks why bad things happen to good people who dedicate themselves to serving the Lord. My answer to that is that it is not God who is against me/you; it is the devil who lurks this earth looking for souls to devour. Through his evil ways he waits for those of us with a heart for God to get angry and turn from our faith. Protecting our peace during times such as this is pertinent to how we come out of this on the other side. Will you walk this earth angry, allowing the devil to steal all your joy? Will you crumble and no longer seek God's will for your life because you feel forsaken? Will you blame God for what happened? How will others see your faith walk through this time? Encouraging others during a time such as this means I first had to walk through it. In my case I am walking through that valley at this exact moment. That was the reason for writing this book while I was grieving. I needed to be true to myself and others on what this looks like and how it is okay to grieve, just grieve through grace.

As a youth director, I have a lot of eyes and ears on me. However, most importantly I have God watching over me. If I turned to alcohol rather than scripture, I would be covering up my pain with a consumable item that harms my body. If I turn to watching a sermon, listening to uplifting worship music, dive into scripture, or doing a daily devotion I am consuming words that will give me strength and soak into my blood stream in such a powerful way. Those words will carry me through the day. I will then renew that strength the following day. The bottle of alcohol will carry me through for two hours possibly, cause my actions to create more sadness and regret, and yes, enter my blood stream but only to harm my organs. Each day I am doing my best to make a positive stride forward and face a challenge that I know will be hard to overcome in the absence of my daughter. Today I went back to Sunday service at church, mainly because my granddaughter begged me to go. Knowing she needed her church friends and that the Holy Spirit was pushing her spirit to yearn for church allowed me to see that I was ready for that step. As I drove to church, I felt anxiety over any questions or breakdowns that may happen. As we arrived, I wanted to drive around to the back of the church and sneak in through a back door to be unseen. My spirit said no to that option, and I parked in the front parking lot, stepped out of my car, and slowly walked towards the building. I felt like eyes were all on me when they were not. I felt like my sadness was like a mask on my face and one that I wouldn't want the kids or youth to see on me. In my mind I know that it is healthy for them to see people sad; however, as their mentor and leader I want to set the best example of what grieving through grace looks like. We were greeted by a lot of love and hugs from our amazing church family. A poster hung in the youth classroom where my daughter had taught with words of encouragement and memories from the students. Knowing and seeing the positive difference my daughter was making gives such peace to my heart. Although church was hard and I did end up crying, through 80% of it I needed that.

Facing the giant of grieving in front of others was what I needed. My church needs to be my safe place and where I am refueled for another week to come. My grandbabies need to be there and feel the love surrounding them as well. I have faced my first week back and my second time will be slightly easier and so forth. My faith must show during good times and bad times, during celebrations and during tragedy. I teach in youth ministry of walking in faith, and I am now showing them what walking in faith looks like. They too will have many trials and tribulations throughout life, and I pray that I can set an example of how we allow God to walk with us through these valleys. Advice for day twenty is to allow yourself to face those giants ahead of you and know that many firsts must take place. They won't be easy and most likely some will seem impossible to do if you are thinking in your flesh. Allow the Holy Spirit to walk you through them. Think of each of these hard situations like a rain cloud that you are under. Some are huge storm clouds and some barely have a mist. The only way to get out from under them is to start moving out of their way. Some storms move on quickly and some last a while. Some are like hurricanes and are predictable many days in advance and others come suddenly. During the storm, God is your umbrella of protection. The SON will appear as you seek Him and shine brightly for all to see.

Today marks twenty-one days since I haven't been able to see, speak to, or call my daughter. I can't say that it has gotten any easier with time passing; however, I can say that as time passes, I am learning different coping skills that help me throughout my day. I have never grieved like this before, I have never lost a child before, I have never had such a hole in my heart, so I am learning as I go. Some situations in life you have to have gone through to truly understand how another person can be feeling. In the past when I heard of a parent losing a child my heart would hurt for them, I would pray, and always say I can't imagine the pain that parent is going through. Now I see it is a pain unlike any other. One that leaves you feeling helpless. If human bodies came with remote controls, you would choose first to rewind and not have to lose your loved one, but if you must go through it then you would choose to be put on pause. A long lingering pause where only after time would it automatically turn back on. The numb feelings that are intertwined with high and low emotions are like a computer board on fire. All the nerve endings in my brain seem to be crisscrossed and touching at the ends with no clear signal on how to feel. Today I had to go to my daughter's car and remove some items. Two of the items that stopped me in my tracks were first a watch of hers. As I stared at her watch and the secondhand ticking on and on and on, all my mind could think about was the fact that here is this watch that she would wear around her wrist to watch her day pass by. Now here sits this watch still ticking, the days are still passing, but she is not in them. Life is still going on, this earth is still rotating, but life seems to stand still even though the watch in front of me clearly makes me aware that time is passing by and does not stand still. The second item that caught my eye was my daughter's journal. She loved to get up in the morning, grab a cup of coffee (just like her mother) and just journal her thoughts. I am so extremely thankful that for years she did this because I am able to read her thoughts and her feelings. Some of her journal entries make me cry, some make me laugh, some make me wonder. There is something about her handwritten notes, even in her handwriting from day to day I can feel her emotions. She has letters to her two children in there and I plan to tear those out and get them framed for them to hang in their rooms. Technology has stolen that personal touch of taking a paper and pen and writing down your thoughts. One of my favorite hobbies is

What ~~do~~ is my purpose.

My purpose is to be the best version of my SELF. My purpose is to be the best expression of who I am. My purpose is to teach others and show them a new way. My purpose is to LOVE on people. My purpose is to help and heal people. My purpose is to let Gods will shine through me. My purpose is to share a message, to share my thoughts, knowledge and vision. My purpose is to connect with peoples soul's. SOUL TALK to write a handwritten letter/card and mail it off to someone. I think my daughter picked up on this trait from me and she would be so happy to know that all those years of taking time to put life on paper is our way of having her here with us in a way. Materialistic items have never been on the forefront of my mind. I really could care less if something is worth money or not. It is the meaning behind the item in hand. Her journal is worth more than all the money in the world to me. I have a coffee cup that she would use daily and was one of her favorite cups, and knowing that her hands wrapped around that cup is what means so much to me. The advice I would give for day twenty-one is to be cautious on what you choose to cherish. Cherish memories, cherish videos/pictures, look for ways that your loved one left an imprint of their life whether that be through writing, singing, playing music, painting, etc. and let the other material items go. Family members fight over and ask for things of worth. They seek financial gains; however, nothing worth cherishing should have a dollar amount set to it.

Day twenty-two and most calls, texts, cards, and daily check-ins have come to a holt. People's lives have all went on. The answers of, "I'm not okay," are getting tiresome for many. Yet this is just the beginning of a lifetime of loss for me. I don't expect people to sit by my side or to interrupt their lives for my tragedy. Being the person who has a blank stare a lot of the time and little response has never been me. Through these past twenty-two days I have felt my personality change, not by choice. The curiosity of will I ever be the person I once was is quickly answered with, "No." There is no way to be the same person when someone who was part of me is gone, along with them dying so did a piece of me. In saying this I don't choose to walk around with a grim face or angry at the world in any way. God has a purpose for me still being here and spreading negativity is not what He has intended for me. My numb face or silence quickly breaks at the smile of a child, puppies playing, watching my grandbabies play, enjoying the peace in nature, and many other instances. Walking in grace is walking with your head held high and being grateful for the Heaven that has been created for us. The why questions that run through my head continuously can only be silenced with my faith answer of, I won't have an answer to that until I am in Heaven one day. This is not easy to accept, and I seek to find answers to a question that won't bring my daughter back. Shame and guilt try to settle in as well. A quick reminder from the Holy Spirit alerts me to be aware of this tactic by the devil. Not only is he happy to see my pain, but nothing would also make him happier than to kick me while I'm down and tell me through my thoughts that I could have prevented this from happening. This is a warfare that God must fight for me, and I have confidence that He will bring an army of angels to fight. He is surrounding me with His protection if I rely on His guidance, and I continue to seek grace through this grieving.

Today we found a clear plastic container with a green lid on it. There were items wrapped in newspaper inside. As we unraveled the paper, we saw the porcelain dolls that my husband/her dad had given her every year at her birthday until she was 16 years old. A little back story on that is when he started giving her these dolls, they were found in a Hallmark store. They looked biracial and that was hard to find. So, my husband was so afraid he wouldn't be able to find them year after year until she turned 16 that he actually went and bought all of them. He stored the dolls in his closet and gave them to her one at a time. She would literally sleep with them at night. Most little girls want to sleep with a babydoll or stuffed animal but ours wanted to sleep with a porcelain statue. Each night we would tell her they were going to break but she would beg us to sleep with not just one but two of them. So, we would let her choose two dolls to sleep with knowing that they would clank together in the bed at night and be broken in the morning. Year after year we would glue their heads, arms, or the birthday numbers back on them. You could see thick glue lines where they were put back together. Seeing these dolls brought back so many memories of our precious baby girl. Unfortunately, as we unwrapped the newspaper, only three out of eighteen were still intact. Some in two pieces and others in ten or more pieces. As I stand in tears today, my husband looks at them and says we can put these back together. As I look and see a million broken pieces of what resembles how I feel about my baby's death, he can see hope. He sees how what looks broken is not. As I sit her journaling, this reminds me of how God's great plan is not broken. Every one of us is only here temporarily and he let me borrow her from Him for 29 years. Those 29 years were a blessing and a gift. She is now with her creator. I am so grateful for the husband I have who shows me a different way to see what I don't see at first. Those dolls that he bought so many years ago have given purpose and a lesson to my heartbreak that God pointed out to me. My day twenty-two advice is to see the whole picture and not the broken pieces of God's plan. Know that we don't ever know how long our story will be and what type of literature will be written through our lives. Some of us will live out a love story, some a drama, some a comedy, and some a scary story. We don't know how many chapters are in our story or our loved one's stories. Therefore, I encourage you to not carry around hate, judgement, unnecessary stress, and worry. Fill your heart with compassion and love. Find purpose every day because there is a reason you woke up today.

Lastly, even during the toughest of storms in life we are covered by our Lord and Savior if we just call on Him.

Twenty-three days and a lifetime to go. My sweet daughter went to be with Jesus. When I first came home from the hospital the day that she passed I was so afraid I wouldn't be able to look at all the pictures on my walls without pure sadness running through my veins. I have found though that her pictures give me joy. I have many photos of her around my home and I stare at her with peace knowing she is with God. She had a heart of gold and loved the Lord. I see in her face years of memories that I was able to cherish with her. Her material items are still hard for me but in them as well I find comfort.

Today I was washing a load of her clothes, mind you my daughter had a passion for shopping just like I do. I taught her well because this child of mine has enough clothes to open a clothing store. When she and I were stressed, we would say we needed shopping and coffee therapy.

Those were our favorite times. The two of us could find a deal like no other on almost everything. The only difference is her style was spot on; she was stunning from head to toe. My style is that of a grammy. I literally have a sweater tree instead of a coat tree in my home. As I was folding her laundry so that I can put it in bins for her daughter when she gets older, I came across a sweatshirt. This sweatshirt has a story behind it. One day we had met for lunch, and she showed up wearing a grey sweatshirt with lace running down the sleeves and I just so happened to show up wearing a mauve sweatshirt with lace running down its sleeves. We were shocked to see that we had both bought the same sweatshirt and had no knowledge of the other one doing so. I asked her where she had bought hers and she bought hers at a store close to her home at a bargain store and I bought mine from a completely different town in a different bargain store. As you know bargain stores sell random items and usually only one or two of each item, so this rare occurrence was so shocking to us but was such a special moment to see how much we were alike. We would randomly show up on certain days wearing those same sweatshirts and would just laugh. In finding this sweatshirt in the wash, I just stood there clenching it with my hands and hugging it tightly. Those small moments are what keeps her feeling present today even though I know she is not here with me. A piece of her lives inside of me in my mind and in my heart and always will. My day twenty-three advice is to take time to let yourself process and seek joy out of the memories you have. Think back to the funny stories or look through pictures and reminisce on the amazing soul your loved one was. We don't need to focus on the bad thoughts or what our loved one might have done throughout the years to upset us. Put your focus on the good times you had and the attributes that leave an amazing legacy behind. As a forewarning, there will be people in your life that will bring up negativity about your loved one, and if you're like me you will want to chop them in the throat. However, their ignorance is only the devil once again trying to steal your joy. Shut down those conversations quickly by stating you are only listening to positive words and if they are not able to honor that then you cannot communicate with them at this time. Protect your peace, don't step out of character of who God has created you to be due to the evil in this world.

Continuing to move forward twenty-four days later. Yes, maybe I am the turtle in this race and moving at the slowest speed forward possible, but I am moving and that's what matters. Do not be in a race to grieve quickly or move on quickly. Sitting still has never been my forte; I am simply not good at it. My plate in life always looks like Thanksgiving. I continue to heap it on more and more until it all mixes together like a humongous smorgasbord. There are friends in my life that remind me or call me out during this time when my eyes are bigger than my stomach, or should I say my will is bigger than my strength right now. There is no need to rush back into a full schedule and trying to help others when I need to allow myself time to heal. I am finding that I am easily annoyed when someone walks in a room smiling and laughing and asks how I am. These feelings are simply coming from the fact that I am still wanting to say, "I am NOT OKAY!" Another part of me almost feels guilty for dragging down the mood of the room or even just the individual who is happy by my somber attitude. Learning to accept that my feelings are justified in this instance, and I don't have to be the life of the party is a task for me. In general, I am a very upbeat person with an extremely positive attitude in most cases. Therefore, this new me, this sad me, this angry me, is an uncomfortable feeling.

My day twenty-four advice is accepting the changes in your personality if they don't alter your thoughts about yourself in an unhealthy manner. Sadness, anger, numbness are all what is to be expected. Don't be ashamed of your emotions. Allow others to be happy and understand they are living life and you are grieving deeply and that is to be expected.

Twenty-five days of thinking twenty-four hours a day about my daughter. Grieving is a battle of the mind and complete exhaustion has set in. When I say I think about her twenty-four hours a day, those thoughts include my heart missing her so much it hurts, as well as all the memories we had together good and bad. Being her mom means we went through times when being her friend wasn't an option, but I always loved being the person God chose me to be, and that was her mom. Someone I was talking to a few days ago had said something profound and it has been really on my mind. What she said was sometimes God takes people to Heaven before we think they should be taken from us because He knows their heart. We went on to discuss how it is so hard to wrap our heads around young lives being taken. However, if given the choice between living for 90 years and not having salvation or living for 29 or less years and having everlasting life, it is a simple answer as to what would be chosen. There is a chance that God knew my daughter's heart and knew she was right with Him at this moment. God can also see into the future and possibly her heart could have turned from Him if given time to do so seeing as evil lurks around looking for souls to devour. In looking at this tragedy through the lens of that magnifying glass, I am given peace in God's purpose of His timing. Death has no hold on a

Christian heart. Death is a door to Heaven for those that have accepted Jesus Christ as their Lord and Savior.

My heart breaks for those souls that do not know God. I pray deeply for them to turn to Him before their timeline on this earth is up. We only have till that last breath to accept Him, not a second longer. Younger generations today often teeter on the spiritual end of their beliefs. Teetering can often equal wavering and the Bible is crystal clear and as pure as it can be when we are given instructions on how to live. We all ask what our purpose is continuously. Love is our purpose! Love others and lead them to Christ so they can have eternity.

Everything else in life comes after that very fact. Live by example not by judgement. God will be the judge. Teach wisdom and discernment. Today I took my eleven-year-old granddaughter to the mall and she wanted to walk through one of the stores as we were passing by. We entered the store and walked down one aisle and turned to me and said, "I don't want these bad spirits on me, we need to leave." We immediately left the store and I explained to her that the feeling she felt was the Holy Spirit giving her discernment of right and wrong and she was so wise to listen to it.

It is approaching fall and so stores are filled with Halloween items that seem to become more and more gruesome and evil based as the years go by. I love fall, I love pumpkins, I love the crisp air, and everything that comes along with the seasonal change from summer to fall. My whole life I have enjoyed Halloween as well. When I was a little girl, I was raised in the suburbs of Chicago. We had tree lined streets and sidewalks. The homes weren't big but felt just perfect to me. I lived in the same house until I was fourteen years old. Every Halloween we would walk home from school and go trick-or-treating with all our neighbor friends. My two sisters and I would then go back to our house and pour all our candy on the ground and sort it out. We would sit for hours trading candy. This was one of my favorite times of the year. When my children were little, I would dress them up each year and take them as well. I remember one year hand sewing a Pebbles and BamBam costume for April and her brother and they won a costume contest at the neighborhood park for their cuteness. The thought never really crossed my mind of the backstory or meaning behind Halloween. A few years ago, my mom and older sister decided to not take part in Halloween traditions of trick-or-treating on Halloween. Each year I have continued going trick-or-treating with my grandbabies. My discernment has been alerting me more and more to the wickedness that the stores and public have turned it into. This year we will not be taking part in Halloween. I will be taking part in fall festivities, however. I now have my daughter's two children to lead by example. Each generation needs to be better than the last and I want to teach them from a young age to have that discernment that it took me years and years to listen to.

My day twenty-five advice is to listen to that small voice within you. Quiet the noises in your head and know that your loved one is in a place of peace if he/she loved the Lord. We all have a stopwatch attached to our lives and we don't know when it will be up so stay prepared spiritually. Listen to the discernment given to you and seek out those who you know are struggling with having a relationship with the Lord and love them just as we are instructed to do.

Day twenty-six, we went to spend an evening with a few very close friends of ours. They are a young couple in their thirties and have two young children. Two years ago, the husband was diagnosed with ALS and given two to four years to live. This was devasting news to a perfectly healthy-looking young man. We have walked through this difficult time with them. There are no words to make it better, there are no medicines or cures to heal him, and he has been saying goodbye to his wife and kids now for years. As we sat with them this evening, we shared how we are walking through the death of our daughter with grace. We explained how we are walking in the Holy Spirit and not in our flesh. Knowing that our flesh is not capable or strong enough for the situation at hand. We encourage them to take videos and pictures. Take pre-recorded videos for future graduations, weddings, or huge milestones. Each second is an opportunity for memories to still be made. We lost our daughter suddenly with no forewarning to get to say goodbye, I love you, or give her one last hug. We also didn't have to watch her suffer, be in pain, or make decisions to prolong life. No timing is right timing. Whether you know the roundabouts of your timeline or if you have no forewarning, it is still going to be reality for all of us at some point. What most people don't consider is that we are all on a timeline and it most likely won't be even a hundred years.

When our daughter passed away, she left behind her two children ages seven and eleven. I am extremely close to both and always have been. Now that she is gone, I look for signs within them to see how they are emotionally doing. I have noticed one of them currently really needing me right by her side. Today she shared with me that she is scared to lose me too.

This is a normal reaction to having just lost her mother. I can't tell her nothing will ever happen to me. My response to her is that Jesus knows what she needs, and He knows that I am raising her; therefore, we must trust that He will allow me to do so. I watch my words so that what I say won't cause them to turn from God if I make a promise that I have no control over. When my daughter passed, I knew that my grieving would have to take place around the grieving and needs of her children. In addition, I know that I am an emotional creature whereas my husband and sons are not. I check in on them as well. My husband has been my rock throughout this tragedy. Setting his own emotions to the wayside. Many people around me are also suffering,.I am not strong enough to hold them all up. However, I am strong enough to listen and sit and pray with them. I am strong enough to go through scripture and explain God's plans for our lives. I am strong enough to still be the hands and feet of Jesus if He calls on me during this time. All of this is possible because He will give me the strength needed. He will not leave me nor forsake me. He will carry me when I am too weak to walk, and He will place me down gently where I need to be and who I need to be with. As I embark on this journey of grief daily, I know God is using my testimony to help others that are going through or will be going through this as well. My day twenty-six advice is to hang on tight to God's word. Let Him be the harness that is holding you up not loosely but as tight as possible. Allow others to see your walk and see your fight but also your spiritual weapons you are fighting with.

Twenty-seven days have come and gone. My sunglasses have been a new fashion statement so that my puffy eyes from crying won't show. A friend of mine had said I looked refreshed the other day. Believe it or not. it was a bit humorous since I think refreshed meant make-up less and like I just woke up from a long winters nap. People are very complimentary when they know someone is going through such tragedy. I hear a lot that I am so strong, I am handling everything so well, it's so good to see me laugh, I look refreshed, and so on. Inside the weakness is a battle, the urge to stay in bed even after twenty-seven days is a battle, and finding happiness in all the moments that my daughter is not able to be there is unbearable. That is the reason I walk not in flesh but in the Holy Spirit.

I was raised on the south side of Chicago. The lesson of finding friends who could defend you and have your back was a life skill that I had mastered. My teenage mouth and attitude along with my red head anger was not a good match for puberty. I thought I was invincible and could take on the world's biggest giants. In reality I weighed 110 pounds and was a child who was looking for trouble. Teenagers think the whole world is up against them. When you were young the simple fact that you didn't get to go to the mall with your friends was a travesty. Then you become an adult and quickly the realization of what a true battle is sets in. All those friends that had my back when I was younger are far and few at this stage in the game. The few amazing friends I have would still have my back if I needed them to. The issue at hand is that the battles I am up against are not able to be rectified with words or actions. The battles that I endure, especially the one I am in right now, can only be battled by my one best friend. This best friend has my back in a way no other can. This best friend established an army many years ago just for my battles. This best friend sacrificed Himself for me and my sins long before I was even born. So, when I need my battle to be fought, I step back and allow the army standing behind me to step forward, put up their shields, and go to war on my behalf. I need not try to fight this giant because God is fighting on my behalf, and He is the mighty warrior.

God will win the battle; however, battles take time. Patience and stamina will carry me through as I wait on the Lord to wave the flag of victory over this battle. Taking down the giants of fear, anger, resentment, and sadness will take time. Each weapon formed against me will be overcome by my Lord and Savior. The Bible clearly states in Isaiah 54:17, "No weapon formed against thee shall prosper; and every tongue that shall rise against thee in judgement thou shalt condemn.

This is the heritage of the servants of the Lord, and their righteousness is of me, saith the Lord." The advice for day twenty-seven is to cling to the words of that scripture. The Bible does not tell a lie; it only makes promises. Read that scripture daily; store those words up in your heart. Then step back and allow God to fight this battle for you.

Day twenty-eight, today I started my day with coffee and listening to a sermon. Since my daughter passed, there seems to be a lot of sermons or scriptures put in front of me that relate to healing. Healing that can be performed by a simple word or touch from God. When these sermons or scriptures are presented to me, there seems to be a feeling of anger or frustration that comes over me. God will present our struggles to us in a way that will allow us to heal through them and see the meaning behind what we can't understand. We tend to fight our flesh. Anger is an emotion that settles in when we don't use scripture to rebuke it. However, in the instance that the scripture is a factor that triggers anger we must dive deeper into scripture to rebuke those emotions. When I sat in that hospital room with my daughter wailing and begging for God to heal her, I didn't understand why my child wasn't chosen for a miracle. Why are some people chosen and others not? I live my life according to God's word, I lead others to God, and am a God-fearing woman. Why would this be happening to me?

Some questions are left to be unknown. Faith in God's decision to take her home to be with Him is a fact that I must understand is not for me to have an answer to. As I look further into scripture, I am reminded that this earth is temporary. This earth is not our final destination and at some point, we all leave here to be either with our creator or in hell. My daughter is in a place of peace. She feels no pain, no sorrow, no suffering. She is in a place every Christian is attempting to live their life trying to go to. She is in a place where the devil can no longer tempt or taunt her. She is protected by the greatest power ever. If you could place your children's lives in the hands of someone who can give them eternal life of no suffering and complete peace unselfishly, that is what you would choose for them. It is so scary being a parent. We do everything we can to teach them right from wrong, good from evil. As our children approach ages of temptation, we pray so hard they will make Godly decisions. We must sit back and watch the repercussions of their actions take place. We pray those seeds we planted while they were young took root and will grow past the weeds of temptation of worldly acts of evil. I have raised three children to adulthood. It has not been an easy feat. Some years were easier than others and to be honest it was much easier when they were young children. My husband and I could control the environment they were in and the influences on their lives. We could choose their friends and give them a curfew. Once they became adults, we had to have faith that we did what we could in those eighteen years to achieve a well planted and watered seed within them. Just like any seed planted, there are times of growth, times of drought, and times of blooming. We go through each of those seasons if there was an initial seed of salvation planted. My day twenty-eight advice would be to put on your overalls and gardening gloves and start planting seeds in salvation in those around you. Having peace in knowing the ones you love will have everlasting life is the greatest reward anyone could ever ask for.

Day twenty-nine was a day of chaos. Beginning a day with three puppies and two children to get ready, fed, and out the door before 8:00 a.m. is a recipe for pure chaos. In raising grandchildren, we wake them up much differently than we did our first three children. I attempt to wake them with my grammy voice. I then gently shake their shoulders. Ten minutes later I return and the grammy voice has turned into the mom voice that is elevated and is now barking to get out of the bed and get dressed.

In the meantime, we have three puppies. Yes, I said three. Before our daughter passed, my husband was working at a job where he fell in love with a puppy. When it was time to take home the puppy he chose, he soon realized that the sister needed a home as well. He didn't want to separate them so needless to say Marvin and Mocha became part of our home. They are five months old and haven't realized that going to the bathroom in the house is a no-no. When our daughter passed, we took in her puppy as well. He was her baby and she loved him dearly. Rocco is a one-year-old pocket bully and he is a great dog. His only downfall is that he is Houdini and escapes cages. He breaks the locks right off. However, he also must be near someone at all times so when we leave him alone at home out of a cage, he throws a fit and today he ate through a box of juice boxes and went to the bathroom on the floor. To top it all off, it rained last night and that equals mud outside. We have twelve paws that run through it and back into the house onto the cream-colored rugs. One trip around the living room equals hundreds of dog prints. I finally got all the dogs fed and taken out to then be matched with two grandchildren who are now upset they must get ready to go so early. Homeschooling is an amazing way to educate your children. However, kids who are homeschooled and parents who homeschool do not think eight in the morning is daytime. That is considered nighttime. Ten o'clock in the morning is when we function. We made it out of the house and embarked on our day. As I was driving down the winding country road back to my house, I was listening to a Christian radio station. The song I was listening to was repeating how God is still on the throne just as the song was singing those words two other radio stations were interrupting it and blending in. The sound of muffled voices and chaos rang through my speakers with no clarity. As I would turn a corner, I would attempt to hear the Christian song I was listening to, but it was so hard to hear the words being sung. Once I arrived home it was clearly playing again. As I sat in my car, the thought came to me that in days of chaos such as today, we must seek to find the Lord. Just like the radio stations that attempted to muffle the words I needed to hear life will do the same. The world will attempt to muffle God so that I cannot hear Him. The world will throw things at me that will make it seem like God is not there. But my God, my Lord, my Alpha & Omega sits on the throne yesterday, today, and always. We must continue to seek him and wait out those muffled times so that when clarity comes back through, we are eagerly awaiting to hear from Him. The advice I have for day twenty-nine is to seek the clarity of the Lord in all circumstances. As the devil tries to muffle your mind with confusion stay steadfast in those moments and wait out the storm. God will resurface and calm the circumstance.

 How did thirty days pass without me being able to hear my daughter's voice? I have prayed for her to visit me in a dream or visit me in spirit. I continuously seek to find ways to connect with her and know she is okay. As parents we always want to hear that our children are okay and happy. As these thirty days have passed by, a lot has not been mentioned. We have had many questions surrounding the circumstance in which our daughter passed away. For thirty days I have walked around with anger in my heart not knowing if foul play was involved. Today I chose peace! I am letting go of what is holding my heart back from healing. When anger settles into your heart, all aspects of your life are being held back by restraints. Those restraints have been cut off today. For me to move forward, I have chosen to hand it all over to God. I don't have to carry that load because He willingly takes it for me if I just hand it over to Him. The choices I make are based off my mental health, my physical health, and most importantly my spiritual health. The devil would love nothing more than to hold me in this negative mind space knowing that I cannot fulfill God's purpose for my life while in this emotional state. Moving forward does not equal me forgetting. Moving forward does not mean the hole in my heart is filled that my daughter has with her in heaven.

    Moving forward does not mean life will be back to what it was before her death. I am choosing to move forward with her by my side in spirit. I see her in her children, in myself, and all around me. Her legacy will live on forever and she will never be forgotten. Letting go of the questions and the anger does not release me from sadness. The emotion of sadness will remain with me forever. Knowing my daughter is gone is the saddest tragedy that has ever happened to me. This order of life's cycle is out of order and no parent should have to bury their child. None of us know our timing or our loved one's timing. What I do know is that when my time is up to be reunited with my daughter in heaven there will be a huge celebration. I have no idea what that looks like seeing as I have not been there. The Bible is my hope into my eternal life, and everything described regarding heaven is a place we will all want to be. It is a place created just for us by God our Father's hands. Heaven will lack nothing and will be perfect. In knowing what the Bible says, I can only be filled with joy knowing that my baby girl is in such a glorious place. Thirty days ago, I would not have been able to let go of the anger and all I wanted was answers. Those answers are still unanswered. However, after thirty days of grieving through grace, I now simply seek peace. I am so grateful for a God that will take on my burdens for me and is the ultimate judge. No matter what is known or unknown here on this earth God knows all and sees all. Ecclesiastes 12:14 states, "For God shall bring every work into judgement, with every secret thing, whether it be good, or whether it be evil." That verse releases me from having to take on the role of cop, judge, detective, and investigator. My role is to be a Christian woman of God that follows His lead. Many things in this life will not be understood. Many unanswered questions regarding death will cause strife and anger. Those emotions are a choice to carry around with you and if you allow them to be they will become your burden.

A month has passed and the advice I would give to you is to seek grace in all things, leave the things you have no control over to God, refrain from allowing the devil to steal your joy.

My prayer for each one of you reading this book is for God to send the Holy Spirit to place peace and comfort in your heart. Thirty days ago, I was unable to fathom how I would get through this tragedy. All my many emotions are supported and justified. How I walk through this event will determine my mental and physical well-being for my future. In knowing that God has a purpose for me and my daughter's children I can live out each day. My daughter will never be forgotten, and I will think of her every day for the rest of my life. There is no way to fill that hole in my heart. The choice to walk in peace and grace is a decision I will make daily.

My two grandchildren are a piece of April still here on this earth with me. Daily they will be encouraged to walk in grace as well. As we woke up today my grandson and I had a discussion of how we are here on this earth because God has work that needs to be done. Our job is to love one another and lead others to Christ. He made me so proud when he said I want to do something for others. He said he wants to give blankets to the homeless people. At seven years old he is following the Holy Spirit within himself and showing how even in this time of loss we can still think of what others need. He is naming his foundation Hugs from Heaven in remembrance of his mom. She often told me when she would be in her car with him, and they would see a homeless person he always begged to stop and get them food. So, she would go get something for them to eat and bring it back to them. She didn't realize at that time, but she taught him a special kind of love. That will be a part of him always. What we do is more significant than we think. She would be so proud to know he is going to show compassion to others throughout life because of her influence.

This book has been created during a moment of real emotion, real grieving, and real pain. No filters, no unrelatable feelings. As I continue to walk through this process of grief, I might have times where these first thirty days of advice on how to grieve must be repeated. Be aware that there may be a week, month, months, or years that go by, and a time of deep mourning settles back in. Pull this book back out, remind yourself it's okay to not be okay. Someone you loved and was a piece of you will not be here on earth with you again for your lifetime. That is not something you will ever get over. You will learn to cope and grieve through grace. You will never be the same because a hole this big doesn't get filled with anything sufficient. There is nothing you can turn to other then God who can hold you up and send you peace through the Holy Spirit. Nothing on this earth can or will ever be able to give you what God can. Tap into that Holy Spirit power and set aside the flesh that is fighting against you. Walking in grace simply means giving yourself up to God to fill your lungs with His breath, your mind with His word, and give yourself grace to grieve!

This book has been written in memory of my daughter April Lynn Holt 1994-2023. She will be forever missed and never forgotten. Heaven gained our angel!

I would love to hear how this book has impacted your walk through the loss of your cherished loved one.

If you feel like sharing your story/want prayer during this time, please reach out to me personally at grievingthroughgrace@gmail.com

John 3:16 "For God so loved the world that he gave his only begotten Son, that whoever believeth in him should not perish, but have everlasting life."